The Biden-Trump Showdown: Partisan Perspectives on Accomplishments

Copyright Page

TITLE: The Biden-Trump Showdown: Partisan Perspectives on Accomplishments

1ST Edition

ISBN: 9798223062493

The Biden-Trump Showdown: Partisan Perspectives on Accomplishments

By Roberto Miguel Rodriguez

Accomplishments of Joe Biden as Seen by Democrats and of Donald Trump by Republicans

Economic Policies: Biden's Job Creation Strategy vs. Trump's Tax Cuts

One of the key differences between Joe Biden and Donald Trump lies in their approach to economic policies. While Trump focused on tax cuts to stimulate economic growth, Biden has proposed a job creation strategy to address the needs of the American workforce.

During his tenure, Trump implemented significant tax cuts, particularly for corporations and high-income individuals. Advocates of Trump's tax cuts argue that they stimulated economic growth, leading to job creation and increased wages. However, critics argue that these tax cuts primarily benefited the wealthy and did not result in substantial improvements for the average American worker.

In contrast, Biden's job creation strategy focuses on investing in infrastructure, renewable energy, and research and development. He believes that these investments will not only create millions of jobs but also address critical issues such as climate change and technological advancements. Biden's plan also includes raising the federal minimum wage to $15 per hour, providing workers with better job protections, and expanding access to affordable healthcare and education.

Supporters of Biden's job creation strategy argue that it will lead to more equitable economic growth, benefiting a broader range of Americans. They believe that by investing in infrastructure and renewable energy, the country can create sustainable, well-paying jobs while addressing urgent environmental concerns. Additionally, they argue that Biden's focus on increasing the minimum wage and expanding access to healthcare and education will lead to a stronger and more resilient workforce.

On the other hand, proponents of Trump's tax cuts argue that they provided businesses with the necessary resources to expand and hire more employees. They believe that reducing corporate taxes and regulations creates a favorable environment for entrepreneurship and investment, ultimately benefiting the American worker.

In conclusion, the economic policies of Biden and Trump differ significantly. While Trump's tax cuts aimed to stimulate economic growth, Biden's job creation strategy focuses on investing in infrastructure, renewable energy, and research. The choice between these two approaches will depend on voters' priorities and their visions for the future of the American economy.

Biden's Focus on Infrastructure Investments

Infrastructure has long been a pressing issue in the United States, with crumbling roads, bridges, and outdated transportation systems hindering economic growth and posing risks to public safety. Recognizing this urgent need, President Joe Biden has made infrastructure investments a top priority of his administration. This section will explore Biden's focus on infrastructure investments and how it differs from the approach taken by his predecessor, Donald Trump.

Under Biden's leadership, the American Jobs Plan was introduced, which aims to modernize the nation's infrastructure and create millions of well-paying jobs. The plan allocates $2.3 trillion to various infrastructure projects, including rebuilding highways, bridges, and railways, expanding broadband access, upgrading water systems, and investing in clean energy initiatives. This comprehensive approach not only addresses the immediate infrastructure needs but also lays the foundation for a more sustainable and resilient future.

In contrast, Trump's approach to infrastructure focused primarily on deregulation and private investment. While he proposed a $1.5 trillion infrastructure plan, it relied heavily on public-private partnerships and tax incentives to attract private investors. Critics argued that this approach would primarily benefit wealthy investors and neglect projects that are not financially lucrative, such as rural infrastructure or low-income communities.

Biden's plan, on the other hand, emphasizes equitable investments that benefit all Americans. It includes provisions to address racial and economic disparities, such as targeting 40% of the benefits to disadvantaged communities. This commitment to inclusivity and social justice sets Biden's approach apart from Trump's more market-driven strategy.

Furthermore, Biden's infrastructure plan is intertwined with his clean energy agenda. By investing in renewable energy, electric vehicles, and energy-efficient buildings, Biden aims to create a more sustainable future while simultaneously creating jobs. This aligns with his commitment to combat climate change and rejoin the Paris Agreement, which Trump withdrew from during his presidency.

In summary, Biden's focus on infrastructure investments represents a significant departure from Trump's approach. Biden's plan prioritizes equitable investments, sustainability, and job creation, while Trump's strategy relied more on private sector involvement. As American voters consider the accomplishments of Biden and Trump, they must evaluate the potential long-term benefits of Biden's infrastructure investments and the positive impact they could have on the economy, the environment, and the lives of all Americans.

Trump's Corporate Tax Reductions

Section: Trump's Corporate Tax Reductions

In this section, we will delve into one of the key economic policies implemented by former President Donald Trump – his corporate tax reductions. These tax cuts were a central component of his administration's economic agenda, aimed at stimulating business growth, job creation, and overall economic prosperity. However, their impact and effectiveness have been subjects of intense debate and partisan divide.

From a Republican perspective, Trump's corporate tax reductions were hailed as a game-changer for American businesses and the economy. The Tax Cuts and Jobs Act of 2017, signed into law by Trump, significantly lowered the corporate tax rate from 35% to 21%, making it more competitive globally. This reduction aimed to incentivize companies to invest, expand operations, and create jobs within the United States. Republicans argue that these tax cuts unleashed economic growth, resulting in increased employment opportunities and higher wages for American workers.

Proponents of Trump's tax cuts also contend that they encouraged businesses to repatriate offshore profits, leading to a surge in domestic investment and infrastructure development. They argue that this influx of capital bolstered industries across various sectors, including manufacturing, technology, and energy, ultimately benefitting American workers and consumers.

However, critics, particularly Democrats, have raised concerns about the long-term consequences of Trump's corporate tax reductions. They argue that these tax cuts disproportionately favored wealthy corporations and the top echelons of society, exacerbating income inequality. They assert that the benefits of these tax cuts were not adequately trickled down to the middle class or low-income individuals.

Furthermore, opponents argue that the revenue loss resulting from these tax cuts has contributed to a ballooning national deficit, compromising the government's ability to fund essential social programs and infrastructure projects. They contend that these tax cuts primarily benefitted shareholders and executives through stock buybacks and dividend payments, rather than driving substantial job creation or wage growth.

As American voters, it is crucial to analyze and evaluate the impact of Trump's corporate tax reductions objectively. By considering the perspectives of both Republicans and Democrats, we can better understand the ramifications of such policies on the economy, job market, income distribution, and overall national well-being.

Impact on Job Growth and GDP

The impact of presidential policies on job growth and GDP is a crucial aspect for American voters to consider when evaluating the accomplishments of Joe Biden as seen by Democrats and Donald Trump by Republicans. The economic policies implemented by each candidate have the potential to shape the nation's prosperity and the livelihoods of its citizens.

Biden's Job Creation Strategy vs. Trump's Tax Cuts

Joe Biden's job creation strategy aims to revitalize the economy by investing in infrastructure, clean energy, and manufacturing. By prioritizing domestic production and reducing reliance on foreign supply chains, Biden intends to create millions of well-paying jobs. This approach emphasizes the importance of supporting American workers and industries.

On the other hand, Donald Trump's tax cuts were aimed at stimulating economic growth by reducing corporate tax rates and providing incentives for businesses to invest. Proponents argue that these tax cuts encouraged job creation and increased GDP. However, critics argue that the benefits primarily favored the wealthy and did not lead to sustained job growth.

Foreign Relations: Biden's Diplomatic Approach vs. Trump's America First Doctrine

Biden's diplomatic approach emphasizes rebuilding alliances and engaging in multilateral cooperation. By rejoining international agreements and organizations such as the Paris Climate Accord and the World Health Organization, Biden aims to strengthen global relationships and promote American interests on the world stage. This approach is seen as a departure from Trump's "America First" doctrine, which prioritized unilateral actions and renegotiating trade deals.

Climate Change: Biden's Clean Energy Agenda vs. Trump's Withdrawal from Paris Agreement

Biden's clean energy agenda focuses on combating climate change by transitioning to renewable energy sources, reducing greenhouse gas emissions, and investing in sustainable infrastructure. This approach aligns with the goals of the Paris Agreement and aims to position the United States as a global leader in addressing climate change.

In contrast, Trump's decision to withdraw from the Paris Agreement was based on the belief that it placed an unfair burden on American industries. Critics argue that this action undermined global efforts to combat climate change and damaged the United States' reputation as a leader in environmental sustainability.

Racial Equality: Biden's Commitment to Social Justice vs. Trump's Law and Order Stance

Joe Biden has made a commitment to addressing systemic racism and promoting social justice. His policies aim to reduce racial disparities in areas such as criminal justice, housing, and education. This includes reforming policing practices and investing in communities disproportionately affected by racial inequality.

Donald Trump's approach to racial equality was centered around a "law and order" stance, emphasizing the need for strong law enforcement and support for police officers. While Trump argued that this approach would ensure public safety, critics argued that it failed to adequately address the underlying issues of racial injustice.

The impact of these policies on job growth and GDP is significant. Biden's job creation strategy focuses on investing in industries that have the potential to stimulate economic growth and create sustainable employment opportunities. By contrast, Trump's tax cuts aimed to stimulate economic growth by reducing corporate tax rates, with the hope that businesses would reinvest in the economy and create jobs.

In terms of foreign relations, Biden's diplomatic approach is expected to restore alliances and promote international cooperation. This could potentially lead to increased trade opportunities and foreign direct investment, which can positively impact job growth and GDP.

Regarding climate change, Biden's clean energy agenda has the potential to create new industries and job opportunities in the renewable energy sector. By transitioning to cleaner and more sustainable energy sources, the United States can reduce its carbon footprint and contribute to global efforts to combat climate change.

Addressing racial inequality is also crucial for job growth and GDP. Biden's commitment to social justice aims to create a more equitable society where opportunities are not limited by race or ethnicity. By investing in communities disproportionately affected by racial inequality, Biden's policies seek to provide equal access to education, employment, and economic opportunities.

In conclusion, the impact of job growth and GDP on these key policy areas is significant. Evaluating the accomplishments of Joe Biden and Donald Trump through the lens of their economic policies, foreign relations, climate change, racial equality, and other key areas will help American voters make informed decisions regarding the future direction of the nation.

Foreign Relations: Biden's Diplomatic Approach vs. Trump's America First Doctrine

In this section, we delve into the vastly different foreign relations approaches adopted by President Joe Biden and former President Donald Trump. Their distinct diplomatic strategies have had a profound impact on America's standing in the global arena.

Under the Biden administration, we witness a significant departure from the "America First" doctrine championed by Trump. President Biden believes in the importance of international cooperation and multilateralism as the pillars of effective foreign policy. He has actively re-engaged with international organizations, such as the United Nations and World Health Organization, to rebuild alliances and tackle global challenges collectively.

Biden's diplomatic approach emphasizes rebuilding alliances and fostering partnerships, recognizing that shared values and cooperation are vital for addressing complex global issues. This is in stark contrast to Trump's transactional approach, which often strained relationships with traditional allies and undermined international institutions.

One notable accomplishment of the Biden administration is the restoration of America's commitment to climate change mitigation. By rejoining the Paris Agreement, President Biden has shown his dedication to fighting the global climate crisis and working with other nations to achieve sustainable solutions. This stands in stark contrast to Trump's decision to withdraw from the agreement, which isolated the United States from the international community's efforts to combat climate change.

Furthermore, President Biden has taken a more nuanced and diplomatic approach to immigration. He has proposed a path to citizenship for millions of undocumented immigrants while also addressing border security concerns. This contrasts with Trump's focus on strict border control measures, including the controversial family separation policy, which drew international condemnation.

In terms of trade policy, Biden has sought to strike a balance between protecting American industries and fostering global economic cooperation. His administration has pursued a more measured approach to trade negotiations, seeking to address issues such as intellectual property theft and unfair trade practices through dialogue rather than unilateral tariffs.

Overall, Biden's diplomatic approach prioritizes collaboration, consensus-building, and re-establishing America's role as a global leader. While Trump's America First doctrine aimed to put American interests first, it often isolated the United States from its traditional allies and undermined its global influence. The divergent approaches of these two presidents have shaped America's foreign relations and will continue to have lasting implications for the country's position on the world stage.

Biden's Multilateral Engagement

One of the defining features of Joe Biden's presidency is his commitment to multilateral engagement. Unlike his predecessor, Donald Trump, who advocated for an "America First" doctrine, Biden believes in the power of collaboration and cooperation with other nations to address global challenges. This approach has been evident in various aspects of his administration, including economic policies, foreign relations, climate change, racial equality, healthcare, immigration, COVID-19 response, education, criminal justice reform, and even the Supreme Court.

In terms of economic policies, Biden's job creation strategy differs significantly from Trump's tax cuts. While Trump's tax cuts were aimed at stimulating economic growth and benefiting corporations and the wealthy, Biden's approach focuses on investing in infrastructure, clean energy, and research and development. By doing so, he aims to create millions of well-paying jobs, bolster the middle class, and ensure a more equitable distribution of wealth.

Biden's diplomatic approach to foreign relations stands in stark contrast to Trump's America First doctrine. Instead of prioritizing national interests above all else, Biden seeks to rebuild alliances, restore America's global standing, and promote democratic values. He has rejoined international agreements such as the Paris Agreement on climate change, the World Health Organization, and the Iran nuclear deal, signaling a commitment to multilateralism and collaborative problem-solving.

The issue of climate change is another area where Biden's agenda differs significantly from Trump's. While Trump withdrew the United States from the Paris Agreement, Biden has made combating climate change a top priority. His clean energy agenda aims to transition to a carbon-free economy, create green jobs, and reduce greenhouse gas emissions. By rejoining the Paris Agreement, Biden has demonstrated his commitment to international cooperation in tackling this global crisis.

Racial equality is another central focus of Biden's presidency. In contrast to Trump's law and order stance, Biden is dedicated to addressing systemic racism and promoting social justice. He has taken steps to advance police accountability, support criminal justice reform, and promote diversity and inclusion in all aspects of society. Through these efforts, Biden aims to create a more equitable and just society for all Americans.

Biden's stance on healthcare also differs significantly from Trump's. While Trump sought to repeal and replace the Affordable Care Act, Biden aims to expand and strengthen it. He believes that healthcare is a right, not a privilege, and has proposed measures to increase access, lower costs, and improve the quality of care for all Americans.

Immigration is another critical area where Biden and Trump have divergent approaches. While Trump focused on border security measures, Biden advocates for a path to citizenship for undocumented immigrants. He has proposed comprehensive immigration reform that provides a pathway to citizenship, strengthens border security, and addresses the root causes of migration.

The COVID-19 response has been a central focus of Biden's presidency. While Trump's Operation Warp Speed focused on developing vaccines, Biden has implemented a comprehensive vaccination plan to ensure the equitable distribution of vaccines across the country. He has also prioritized mask-wearing, testing, contact tracing, and other public health measures to control the spread of the virus and save lives.

In terms of education, Biden's push for free community college differs from Trump's focus on school choice. Biden believes in expanding access to quality education and reducing the burden of student debt. By making community college tuition-free and investing in early childhood education, he aims to provide opportunities for all Americans to succeed and thrive.

Criminal justice reform is another area where Biden's efforts differ from Trump's tough-on-crime approach. Biden advocates for police accountability, ending mass incarceration, and addressing systemic inequalities within the criminal justice system. His administration has taken steps to reform sentencing laws, invest in community policing, and support rehabilitation and reintegration efforts.

Finally, the Supreme Court is an area where Biden's potential expansion differs from Trump's conservative appointments. Biden has expressed openness to expanding the Supreme Court to address concerns about its ideological balance and protect the integrity of the judiciary. This stands in contrast to Trump's focus on appointing conservative justices to the Court.

In summary, Biden's multilateral engagement is a central theme of his presidency. Whether it is economic policies, foreign relations, climate change, racial equality, healthcare, immigration, COVID-19 response, education, criminal justice reform, or the Supreme Court, Biden's approach emphasizes collaboration, cooperation, and a commitment to addressing global challenges through multilateralism. By embracing this approach, Biden seeks to restore America's standing in the world and create a more inclusive, equitable, and prosperous future for all Americans.

Trump's Bilateral Negotiations

One of the key aspects of Donald Trump's presidency was his approach to bilateral negotiations, which aimed to prioritize America's interests above all else. Trump believed in leveraging his business background to negotiate deals that would benefit the American people and strengthen the country's position on the global stage.

In terms of economic policies, Trump's strategy was centered around tax cuts. His administration implemented the Tax Cuts and Jobs Act of 2017, which aimed to stimulate economic growth by reducing corporate tax rates and providing tax relief for individuals. Republicans argue that these tax cuts resulted in increased investment, job creation, and a booming stock market. They believe that Trump's pro-business approach helped to rejuvenate the American economy and benefit workers across various sectors.

Regarding foreign relations, Trump adopted an "America First" doctrine. He prioritized protecting American interests and ensuring that the country was not taken advantage of in international agreements. This approach involved renegotiating existing trade deals, such as the North American Free Trade Agreement (NAFTA), which led to the creation of the United States-Mexico-Canada Agreement (USMCA). Republicans argue that Trump's tough stance on trade and his commitment to fair and reciprocal deals helped to protect American industries and workers.

On the topic of climate change, Trump chose to withdraw the United States from the Paris Agreement. Republicans supported this decision, arguing that the agreement placed an unfair burden on American industries and hindered economic growth. Trump's administration focused on promoting clean energy innovation and reducing regulations that they believed were stifling economic progress.

When it came to racial equality, Trump's emphasis was on maintaining law and order. Republicans argue that Trump's tough-on-crime approach aimed to protect communities and ensure public safety. While Democrats criticized his stance, Republicans believe that Trump's policies were necessary to combat rising crime rates.

In terms of healthcare, Trump made efforts to repeal and replace the Affordable Care Act (ACA). Republicans believed that the ACA was burdensome and led to increased healthcare costs for Americans. Trump aimed to provide more affordable and accessible healthcare options through market-driven reforms.

On the issue of immigration, Trump focused on border security measures. He advocated for stricter immigration policies, including the construction of a border wall. Republicans argue that these measures were necessary to protect national security and prevent illegal immigration.

In response to the COVID-19 pandemic, Trump launched Operation Warp Speed, an initiative aimed at accelerating the development and distribution of vaccines. Republicans credit this program with the rapid development of multiple vaccines and the successful vaccination rollout.

In terms of education, Trump's focus was on promoting school choice. He believed that parents should have the freedom to choose the best educational options for their children, including charter schools and voucher programs. Republicans argue that school choice provides opportunities for students in underperforming schools.

Regarding criminal justice reform, Trump took a tough-on-crime approach. Republicans argue that his policies aimed to protect communities and ensure public safety. However, Democrats criticized his administration for not doing enough to address systemic issues in the criminal justice system.

Finally, Trump prioritized appointing conservative justices to the Supreme Court. Republicans believe that these appointments helped to uphold conservative values and protect the Constitution.

In conclusion, Trump's bilateral negotiations focused on prioritizing American interests and using his business background to negotiate deals that benefited the country. His economic policies, foreign relations approach, and stance on various issues were seen as beneficial by Republicans, who believed that his strategies protected American industries, created jobs, and promoted security and prosperity.

Implications for Global Alliances and Trade

One of the key aspects that will greatly impact the future of the United States is its global alliances and trade relationships. Both Joe Biden and

Donald Trump have had contrasting approaches to these matters, which have significant implications for the country's economy and standing in the international community.

Under Joe Biden, there is a strong commitment to revitalizing global alliances and restoring trust with traditional allies. Biden believes in a multilateral approach, working closely with international organizations such as the United Nations and NATO. His emphasis is on strengthening existing alliances and building new partnerships, with the aim of promoting shared values and addressing global challenges collectively. This approach is likely to result in increased cooperation in areas such as trade, security, and climate change.

Contrastingly, Donald Trump pursued an "America First" doctrine, which often strained relationships with traditional allies. Trump took a more unilateral approach, prioritizing American interests above all else. This led to trade wars with countries like China and the imposition of tariffs on steel and aluminum imports. While Trump supporters argue that these actions protected American jobs and industries, critics argue that they damaged relationships and disrupted global trade.

The implications of these contrasting approaches are significant for the American voters. Biden's focus on rebuilding global alliances and promoting free trade could potentially lead to increased economic opportunities for American businesses and workers. It could also result in greater cooperation in addressing global challenges such as climate change and terrorism.

On the other hand, Trump's America First doctrine may have resonated with some voters who felt left behind by globalization. However, it also came with potential risks, such as trade conflicts and strained relationships with key allies. These consequences could have long-term implications for the American economy and its standing in the world.

As American voters, it is crucial to consider the implications for global alliances and trade when evaluating the accomplishments of both candidates. The decisions made in this area will have far-reaching consequences for the economy, national security, and the country's role on the global stage. It is essential to weigh the potential benefits and drawbacks of each candidate's approach to ensure a prosperous future for the United States.

Climate Change: Biden's Clean Energy Agenda vs. Trump's Withdrawal from Paris Agreement

The issue of climate change has become a defining factor in the political landscape of the United States. It is a topic that has garnered significant attention from both Democrats and Republicans, as it has far-reaching implications for the future of our planet. In this section, we will explore the diverging approaches of President Joe Biden and former President Donald Trump towards this critical issue.

Joe Biden has made tackling climate change a top priority of his administration. He recognizes the urgency of the situation and the need for immediate action. Biden's clean energy agenda centers around investing in renewable energy sources, reducing carbon emissions, and rejoining the Paris Agreement. His vision is to transition the United States to a clean energy economy, creating millions of jobs in the process.

On the other hand, Donald Trump's approach to climate change was marked by his decision to withdraw from the Paris Agreement. This move was met with widespread criticism, as it signaled a lack of commitment to addressing the global climate crisis. Trump's administration also rolled back numerous environmental regulations and supported the fossil fuel industry, which further exacerbated concerns about his stance on climate change.

The contrasting approaches of the two presidents reflect the broader divide between Democrats and Republicans on the issue of climate change. Democrats, like Biden, tend to prioritize environmental protection and sustainable energy solutions. They view climate change as a global threat that requires immediate action and international cooperation.

Republicans, on the other hand, have often been more skeptical of the extent and impact of climate change. They tend to prioritize economic growth and job creation, often at the expense of environmental regulations. However, it is important to note that there are Republicans who do acknowledge the reality of climate change and support efforts to address it.

For the American voters, the choice between Biden's clean energy agenda and Trump's withdrawal from the Paris Agreement represents a fundamental difference in priorities and values. It is a decision that will have long-term consequences for the environment, the economy, and future generations.

Ultimately, the question becomes whether the United States will take a leading role in combating climate change or continue to prioritize short-term economic gains. The answer lies in the hands of the American voters, who have the power to shape the future of our planet through their choice at the ballot box.

Biden's Commitment to Renewable Energy

In recent years, the issue of climate change has taken center stage in global discussions, with the need for sustainable and renewable energy sources becoming more urgent than ever. Joe Biden, the 46th President of the United States, has made it clear that he is committed to addressing this issue head-on and leading the nation towards a clean energy future. His approach stands in stark contrast to that of his predecessor, Donald

Trump, who withdrew the United States from the Paris Agreement and favored a more fossil fuel-dependent energy policy.

Under Biden's leadership, the United States is set to make significant strides in the transition to renewable energy. One of his key initiatives is the Clean Energy Revolution, which aims to achieve a carbon pollution-free power sector by 2035. This ambitious plan includes investing in clean energy research and development, as well as incentivizing the use of renewable energy sources such as wind, solar, and geothermal power. By embracing these technologies, Biden hopes to not only reduce carbon emissions but also create millions of new jobs in the clean energy sector.

Another crucial aspect of Biden's commitment to renewable energy is his focus on rejoining the Paris Agreement. By doing so, the United States will once again be part of a global effort to combat climate change and reduce greenhouse gas emissions. This move signals a shift towards a more collaborative and diplomatic approach to foreign relations, in contrast to Trump's "America First" doctrine.

Furthermore, Biden's commitment to renewable energy is closely tied to his vision of achieving racial equality and social justice. The impacts of climate change disproportionately affect marginalized communities, and Biden recognizes the need to address these environmental injustices. His plan includes investing in disadvantaged communities and ensuring that they have access to clean air, clean water, and clean energy.

While Biden's clean energy agenda is ambitious, it is not without its challenges. The transition to renewable energy will require significant investments and cooperation from both the public and private sectors. However, with his experience and track record of working across party lines, Biden is uniquely positioned to build the necessary coalitions and garner the support needed to make this vision a reality.

In conclusion, Biden's commitment to renewable energy represents a stark departure from Trump's energy policies. By embracing clean energy technologies and rejoining the global effort to combat climate change, Biden aims to create a sustainable and prosperous future for all Americans. His plan not only addresses the urgent need to reduce carbon emissions but also acknowledges the importance of racial equality, social justice, and job creation in the clean energy sector. As American voters, understanding and evaluating this commitment to renewable energy is crucial in assessing Biden's accomplishments and vision for the future.

Trump's Emphasis on Fossil Fuels

Section: Trump's Emphasis on Fossil Fuels

Introduction:

In this section, we will delve into one of the most controversial aspects of Donald Trump's administration - his emphasis on fossil fuels. Trump's energy policies heavily favored the fossil fuel industry, which had a significant impact on the economy, environment, and America's energy future. This section aims to present a Republican perspective on Trump's accomplishments in this area, particularly in contrast to Joe Biden's clean energy agenda.

Trump's Energy Policy:

During his presidency, Donald Trump prioritized the expansion of domestic fossil fuel production, aiming to achieve energy independence and boost job creation in the industry. Under his administration, the United States became the world's leading oil and gas producer, reducing its reliance on foreign energy sources. Trump implemented regulatory rollbacks, such as easing restrictions on coal-fired power plants and offshore drilling, to unleash the potential of the fossil fuel industry.

Economic Impact:

Trump's emphasis on fossil fuels was touted as a way to revitalize the economy and create jobs. The energy sector experienced significant growth, with thousands of jobs added, especially in states like Texas and Pennsylvania. Additionally, reduced energy costs benefited consumers and industries alike, stimulating economic activity across various sectors.

Energy Independence:

Trump's focus on fossil fuels aimed to make the United States energy independent, reducing dependence on foreign oil and enhancing national security. Through increased domestic production, the administration sought to ensure a stable energy supply, safeguarding the nation's interests and reducing vulnerability to geopolitical tensions.

Criticism and Environmental Concerns:

While Trump's emphasis on fossil fuels had its supporters, it also faced criticism from environmentalists and proponents of clean energy. Critics argued that his policies neglected the urgent need to address climate change and transition to renewable energy sources. The rollback of environmental regulations raised concerns about air and water pollution, as well as the impact on vulnerable ecosystems.

Conclusion:

Donald Trump's emphasis on fossil fuels was a defining aspect of his administration's energy policy. While it created economic opportunities and contributed to energy independence, it also faced criticism for its environmental impact. This section provides a Republican perspective on Trump's accomplishments in this area, highlighting the contrast between his approach and Joe Biden's clean energy agenda. As American voters, it is crucial to consider these perspectives and weigh the potential implications for the economy, environment, and the nation's energy future.

Effects on Environmental Sustainability and International Cooperation

The issue of environmental sustainability and international cooperation has become increasingly significant in recent years. Both Joe Biden and Donald Trump have had contrasting approaches when it comes to addressing climate change and promoting international collaboration. This section will explore the effects of their policies in these areas and their implications for the future.

Under Joe Biden's leadership, the United States has witnessed a significant shift towards a clean energy agenda. Biden has pledged to rejoin the Paris Agreement, an international effort to combat climate change, which Donald Trump withdrew from during his presidency. This move demonstrates Biden's commitment to international cooperation and his belief in the importance of collective action in addressing global environmental challenges. By rejoining the Paris Agreement, the United States can once again play a leading role in the global fight against climate change, collaborating with other nations to reduce greenhouse gas emissions and transition to renewable energy sources.

In contrast, Donald Trump's withdrawal from the Paris Agreement signaled a departure from international cooperation on environmental issues. His "America First" doctrine focused primarily on protecting American industries and promoting fossil fuel extraction, which critics argue undermined efforts to combat climate change. Trump's policies, such as rolling back environmental regulations and withdrawing from international climate agreements, raised concerns about the long-term sustainability of the planet and strained relationships with international partners.

The effects of these contrasting approaches are far-reaching. Biden's clean energy agenda not only aims to mitigate climate change but also stands to create new jobs and stimulate economic growth through investments in renewable energy infrastructure. By prioritizing sustainability, Biden seeks to position the United States as a global leader in clean technology and innovation. This could lead to increased international cooperation in the development and implementation of sustainable practices, fostering a greater sense of unity among countries.

On the other hand, Trump's emphasis on fossil fuel extraction and deregulation had short-term economic benefits but potentially detrimental long-term consequences for the environment. By withdrawing from international agreements, the United States risked alienating key allies and undermining global efforts to address climate change. Furthermore, the lack of cooperation on environmental issues could have negative implications for other areas of international collaboration, such as trade and security.

In conclusion, the contrasting approaches of Joe Biden and Donald Trump on environmental sustainability and international cooperation have significant implications for the future. Biden's clean energy agenda and commitment to rejoin the Paris Agreement signal a renewed focus on global collaboration and the pursuit of sustainable practices. In contrast, Trump's "America First" doctrine and withdrawal from international agreements raise concerns about the long-term impact on the environment and relationships with international partners. The American voters must consider these effects when evaluating the accomplishments of Biden and Trump in relation to environmental sustainability and international cooperation.

Racial Equality: Biden's Commitment to Social Justice vs. Trump's Law and Order Stance

In the ongoing battle for racial equality, the differences between Joe Biden and Donald Trump are stark. While Biden champions social justice and equality, Trump's approach has consistently skewed towards law and order. This section will analyze the accomplishments of both candidates in this critical area, shedding light on their respective approaches and the impact they have had on racial equality in America.

Under the Biden administration, the commitment to social justice has been at the forefront of his policies. Biden has consistently acknowledged the systemic racism that plagues our society and has vowed to tackle it head-on. He has promised to address racial disparities in the criminal justice system, promote police accountability, and ensure equal opportunities for all Americans. Biden's commitment to diversity is evident in his nominations for key positions, with an emphasis on representation and inclusivity.

On the other hand, Trump's approach to racial equality has been marred by his law and order stance. His administration's response to protests against racial injustice was often met with force, exacerbating tensions and deepening divisions. Trump's rhetoric, at times, seemed to downplay the significance of systemic racism, leading to further alienation among marginalized communities.

Looking at the accomplishments, Biden has initiated several measures to promote racial equality. He has called for the passage of the George Floyd Justice in Policing Act, which aims to hold law enforcement accountable for misconduct and excessive force. Additionally, Biden has sought to strengthen federal oversight of local police departments and invest in community policing programs. These efforts signify Biden's commitment to reforming the criminal justice system and addressing racial disparities.

In contrast, Trump's focus on law and order has resulted in policies that disproportionately affect minority communities. His administration's strict immigration policies, such as the separation of families at the border, drew widespread condemnation for their impact on immigrant families, many of whom were seeking refuge from dangerous situations.

Furthermore, Trump's refusal to acknowledge the existence of systemic racism and his divisive rhetoric only served to widen the racial divide.

In conclusion, the contrasting approaches of Biden and Trump on racial equality have had a profound impact on the state of social justice in America. Biden's commitment to social justice and equality, as evidenced by his policies and initiatives, has resonated with those who believe in a fair and just society. In contrast, Trump's law and order stance has often perpetuated racial disparities and exacerbated existing divisions. As American voters, it is crucial to consider the accomplishments of both candidates in this area and their implications for the future of racial equality in our nation.

Biden's Support for Police Reform

In recent years, issues surrounding police brutality and systemic racism within law enforcement have become a major concern for Americans across the nation. Joe Biden, as a candidate and now as the President of the United States, has shown a strong commitment to police reform and addressing these pressing issues. His approach stands in stark contrast to Donald Trump's "law and order" stance, making it a significant accomplishment for Democrats and a key point of contention between the two parties.

One of the central pillars of Biden's police reform agenda is the establishment of a national oversight commission. This commission would be responsible for holding law enforcement agencies accountable, ensuring that they adhere to the highest standards of conduct, and investigating cases of misconduct or abuse. By implementing this commission, Biden aims to restore trust between communities and law enforcement, fostering a more equitable and just society.

Another important aspect of Biden's police reform efforts is the push for increased transparency within police departments. He advocates for the mandatory use of body cameras by all law enforcement officers, which would provide an unbiased record of interactions between police and citizens. This measure not only protects the rights of individuals but also serves to hold officers accountable for any misconduct.

Furthermore, Biden recognizes the need for comprehensive training programs that address implicit bias, de-escalation techniques, and cultural competency within law enforcement. By investing in these programs, Biden aims to equip police officers with the necessary tools to navigate complex situations and ensure the safety of both themselves and the communities they serve.

Under the Trump administration, police reform was largely overshadowed by a focus on maintaining law and order. Trump's approach prioritized the support and protection of law enforcement, often disregarding the concerns of marginalized communities disproportionately affected by police brutality. This stark contrast in approach between Biden and Trump highlights the importance of police reform as a critical issue for the nation.

Biden's support for police reform demonstrates his commitment to social justice and equality. By addressing the systemic issues within law enforcement, he aims to create a more just society for all Americans. This accomplishment is viewed favorably by Democrats who believe in the importance of police accountability and the need for comprehensive reform. However, it remains a point of contention for Republicans who argue that Biden's approach may undermine the authority and effectiveness of law enforcement.

In conclusion, Biden's support for police reform is a significant accomplishment from a Democratic perspective. His commitment to establishing a national oversight commission, increasing transparency through the use of body cameras, and implementing comprehensive training programs highlights his dedication to addressing the pressing issues of systemic racism and police brutality. While Republicans may have reservations about the potential impact on law enforcement, it is clear that Biden's efforts are driven by a desire to create a more equitable and just society for all Americans.

Trump's Focus on Crime Prevention

Title: Trump's Focus on Crime Prevention

Introduction:

In this section, we will delve into the accomplishments of Donald Trump, as seen by Republicans, regarding his focus on crime prevention. Trump's law and order stance, along with his tough-on-crime approach, have been key aspects of his administration's policies. This section aims to provide an overview of his initiatives and their impact on crime prevention in the United States.

Reducing Crime Rates:

Donald Trump's presidency placed a strong emphasis on reducing crime rates across the country. Under his administration, efforts were made to combat gang violence, drug trafficking, and illegal immigration, all of which contribute to crime rates. Through stricter border security measures and enhanced cooperation between law enforcement agencies, Trump aimed to create a safer environment for American communities.

Support for Law Enforcement:

Trump consistently expressed his support for law enforcement officers, acknowledging their crucial role in maintaining law and order. He implemented policies that prioritized police funding and equipment, ensuring that officers had the necessary resources to carry out their duties effectively. By promoting a pro-police culture, Trump aimed to empower law enforcement agencies and foster a sense of security within communities.

Criminal Justice Reform:

While Trump's approach was often perceived as tough on crime, his administration also focused on criminal justice reform. The First Step Act, a bipartisan legislation signed by Trump in 2018, aimed to address the issue of mass incarceration and provide better rehabilitation opportunities for non-violent offenders. This landmark legislation emphasized the importance of second chances and reintegration into society.

Combating the Opioid Crisis:

The Trump administration recognized the devastating impact of the opioid crisis on American communities. Initiatives were undertaken to address the crisis through increased funding for prevention, treatment, and recovery programs. By prioritizing resources and implementing stricter regulations on opioid prescriptions, Trump aimed to curb the proliferation of this public health emergency.

Conclusion:

Donald Trump's focus on crime prevention was a significant aspect of his presidency, reflecting his commitment to maintaining law and order in the United States. Through initiatives aimed at reducing crime rates, supporting law enforcement, and implementing criminal justice reform, Trump sought to create safer communities for all Americans. While opinions may vary on his approach, it is important to acknowledge the efforts made during his tenure to address the multifaceted issue of crime prevention.

Impacts on Minority Communities and Criminal Justice System

The impacts on minority communities and the criminal justice system have been a significant focus of debate and discussion in recent years. Both Joe Biden and Donald Trump have had different approaches to addressing these issues, which have had far-reaching consequences for minority communities and the criminal justice system.

Under the Trump administration, the criminal justice system took a tough-on-crime approach, which disproportionately affected minority communities. Trump's law and order stance emphasized harsh punishments and increased police presence, leading to a surge in incarceration rates. This approach did little to address the root causes of crime or promote rehabilitation. Instead, it perpetuated systemic inequalities and widened the racial disparities within the criminal justice system.

In contrast, Joe Biden has long been committed to social justice and police accountability. His efforts for police reform and accountability have been a cornerstone of his criminal justice reform agenda. Biden's push for police reform includes advocating for increased transparency, accountability, and training within law enforcement agencies. He aims to address racial profiling and excessive use of force, which are issues that disproportionately impact minority communities.

Furthermore, Biden's commitment to addressing the root causes of crime extends beyond law enforcement. He recognizes the importance of investing in education, job creation, and economic opportunities for minority communities. By focusing on these areas, Biden aims to break the cycle of poverty and improve outcomes for minority individuals involved in the criminal justice system.

The impacts of these different approaches are significant. Trump's tough-on-crime stance has perpetuated racial disparities and hindered progress towards a more equitable criminal justice system. Biden's commitment to police accountability and addressing systemic inequalities aims to rectify these issues and promote a fairer and more just system.

It is crucial for American voters to consider these impacts when evaluating the accomplishments of Joe Biden and Donald Trump. The criminal justice system plays a pivotal role in shaping the lives of minority communities, and the approach taken by each candidate will have lasting consequences.

The Biden-Trump Showdown provides a unique opportunity for voters to understand and assess the impacts on minority communities and the criminal justice system. By examining the accomplishments and approaches of both candidates, voters can make informed decisions that align with their values and aspirations for a more equitable and just society.

Healthcare: Biden's Expansion of Affordable Care Act vs. Trump's Repeal and Replace Efforts

In the ongoing battle between Democrats and Republicans, one of the most contentious issues has been healthcare. Joe Biden and Donald Trump have offered vastly different approaches to this critical aspect of American life.

On one hand, Biden has vowed to expand the Affordable Care Act (ACA), also known as Obamacare. He believes in building upon the progress made during the Obama administration, ensuring that every American has access to affordable, quality healthcare. Biden's plan includes increasing subsidies, creating a public option, and lowering the age for Medicare eligibility. This expansion aims to provide coverage to the millions of Americans who currently fall through the cracks of our healthcare system.

Trump, on the other hand, has long been a vocal opponent of the ACA. Throughout his presidency, he made numerous attempts to repeal and replace the legislation, arguing that it was costly and ineffective. While he was unsuccessful in fully dismantling the ACA, his administration did manage to chip away at certain provisions, such as the individual mandate. Trump's ultimate goal was to replace the ACA with a new healthcare plan that he promised would be more affordable and accessible to all Americans.

As American voters, we must consider the impact of each candidate's healthcare proposals. Biden's plan seeks to build on the progress made by the ACA, ensuring that millions of Americans have access to the care they need. This expansion could potentially reduce the number of uninsured Americans and provide financial relief to those struggling with high healthcare costs.

Trump's approach, on the other hand, raises concerns about the potential loss of coverage for millions of Americans, particularly those with pre-existing conditions. While he promised a better alternative to the ACA, the lack of a concrete plan during his presidency leaves many skeptical about the potential consequences of his repeal and replace efforts.

Ultimately, the healthcare debate boils down to a fundamental question: should healthcare be a right or a privilege? Biden's expansion of the ACA suggests a belief in the former, while Trump's repeal and replace efforts indicate a more market-driven approach. As American voters, it is crucial that we critically examine each candidate's proposals and consider the potential impact on ourselves, our families, and our communities. Our decision on this issue could have far-reaching consequences for the future of healthcare in America.

Biden's Efforts to Improve Accessibility and Affordability

In his pursuit of a more equitable and inclusive America, President Joe Biden has made significant strides in improving accessibility and affordability for all Americans. From healthcare to education, Biden's policies and initiatives aim to level the playing field and ensure that every individual has the opportunity to thrive.

One area where Biden's efforts stand out is healthcare. Recognizing the importance of accessible and affordable healthcare, Biden has focused on expanding the Affordable Care Act (ACA) rather than repealing it, as his predecessor attempted. By expanding Medicaid and implementing a public option, Biden seeks to ensure that all Americans have access to quality healthcare, regardless of their income or pre-existing conditions.

Education is another key area where Biden has prioritized accessibility and affordability. With a focus on expanding access to higher education, Biden has proposed making community college free for all Americans. By removing financial barriers, Biden aims to provide more opportunities for individuals to gain the skills and knowledge needed for success in the modern economy.

In the realm of immigration, Biden's approach is centered around creating a path to citizenship for undocumented immigrants. Recognizing the contributions of immigrants to our society and economy, Biden aims to provide a fair and accessible process for those seeking to become citizens. This stands in stark contrast to Trump's focus on border security measures, which often resulted in the separation of families and the criminalization of asylum seekers.

Biden's commitment to racial equality is evident in his push for social justice reforms. Recognizing the systemic racism that still exists in our society, Biden has taken steps to hold law enforcement accountable and promote equality in the criminal justice system. This stands in contrast to Trump's "law and order" stance, which often ignored the underlying issues of racial inequality and perpetuated a cycle of injustice.

Furthermore, Biden's efforts to address climate change reflect his commitment to a sustainable and accessible future. By rejoining the Paris Agreement and implementing a clean energy agenda, Biden aims to create new jobs and reduce our dependence on fossil fuels. This is in stark contrast to Trump's withdrawal from the Paris Agreement and his prioritization of the fossil fuel industry.

In conclusion, President Joe Biden's efforts to improve accessibility and affordability highlight his commitment to creating a more equitable and inclusive America. Whether it is expanding access to healthcare, making education more affordable, or promoting racial equality, Biden's policies aim to level the playing field and ensure that every American has the opportunity to succeed. By contrasting his approach with that of his predecessor, it becomes evident that Biden's vision for America is one of accessibility, affordability, and opportunity for all.

Trump's Push for Market-Based Solutions

In the realm of economic policies, President Donald Trump has consistently advocated for market-based solutions to stimulate job creation and economic growth. His approach, centered around tax cuts and deregulation, sought to empower businesses and incentivize investment, ultimately leading to a thriving economy. This section will delve into the accomplishments of President Trump from a Republican perspective and shed light on his strategies that aimed to bolster the American economy.

One of the cornerstones of Trump's economic policies was his signature tax cuts. In 2017, his administration successfully passed the Tax Cuts and Jobs Act, which significantly reduced corporate tax rates and provided relief for middle-class Americans. By reducing the tax burden on businesses, Trump aimed to encourage investment, spur innovation, and ultimately create jobs. These tax cuts were lauded by Republicans as a catalyst for economic growth and a testament to Trump's commitment to free-market principles.

Additionally, Trump's focus on deregulation played a pivotal role in his market-based approach. By reducing government red tape and eliminating unnecessary regulations, Trump sought to empower businesses and remove barriers to their success. This deregulatory agenda aimed to foster innovation, promote competition, and create a business-friendly environment that would attract both domestic and foreign investments.

Trump's economic policies also emphasized fair trade practices and a commitment to American workers. Through renegotiating trade agreements like NAFTA and implementing tariffs on certain goods, Trump aimed to protect American industries and ensure a level playing field for American businesses in the global market.

While Trump's economic policies were met with both praise and criticism, they undeniably had a profound impact on the American economy. Prior to the COVID-19 pandemic, unemployment rates reached historic lows, the stock market soared to record highs, and wages saw significant increases.

In conclusion, Trump's push for market-based solutions in the realm of economic policies was driven by a commitment to free-market principles, job creation, and economic growth. His tax cuts, deregulation efforts, and focus on fair trade practices were all aimed at empowering businesses and fostering an environment conducive to economic prosperity. From a Republican perspective, Trump's accomplishments in this domain serve as a testament to his commitment to market-based solutions and his desire to create a thriving economy for the American people.

Consequences for Healthcare Coverage and Costs

In the ongoing battle between Democrats and Republicans, one key area of contention is healthcare coverage and costs. The consequences of the policies pursued by both Joe Biden and Donald Trump have far-reaching implications for the American people.

Under the leadership of Joe Biden, Democrats have championed the expansion of the Affordable Care Act (ACA), also known as Obamacare. Biden's plan includes increasing the number of people covered by offering a public option, which would provide a government-run insurance plan alongside private options. This would not only ensure more Americans have access to affordable healthcare but also create competition that drives down costs. The expansion of Medicaid would also be a priority, providing coverage to low-income individuals and families who would otherwise struggle to afford insurance.

On the other hand, Donald Trump and Republicans have long sought to repeal and replace the ACA. While they were unsuccessful in fully repealing the law, the Trump administration did manage to dismantle key provisions, such as the individual mandate, which required Americans to have health insurance or face a penalty. This led to an increase in the number of uninsured Americans and put the financial burden of healthcare back on individuals.

The consequences of these differing approaches to healthcare coverage and costs are significant. Under Biden's plan, millions of Americans who currently lack insurance would gain access to affordable healthcare options. This would not only improve the overall health and well-being of individuals but also relieve the burden on emergency rooms, where uninsured individuals often seek care.

In contrast, Trump's efforts to dismantle the ACA had the potential to exacerbate the already high costs of healthcare in the United States. Without the individual mandate, healthy individuals may opt out of purchasing insurance, leaving a smaller pool of insured individuals to bear the costs. This, in turn, drives up premiums for those who remain insured.

Ultimately, the consequences for healthcare coverage and costs are clear. Biden's expansion of the ACA would provide more Americans with access to affordable healthcare, reducing the strain on individuals and improving overall health outcomes. Trump's repeal and replace efforts, on the other hand, would likely lead to higher costs for the insured and leave millions without access to necessary healthcare services.

As American voters, it is crucial to consider the ramifications of these policies on our own lives and the lives of our fellow citizens. The choice between Biden's expansion of the ACA and Trump's attempts to dismantle it has far-reaching consequences that extend beyond political ideologies. It is essential to weigh the impact on healthcare coverage and costs when deciding which candidate's approach aligns with your values and priorities.

Immigration: Biden's Path to Citizenship vs. Trump's Border Security Measures

In the ongoing debate on immigration, the policies of Joe Biden and Donald Trump present two contrasting approaches. For the American voters, understanding the accomplishments of each candidate in this realm is crucial to making an informed decision.

Under President Biden, there is a strong emphasis on creating a path to citizenship for undocumented immigrants. Biden's plan recognizes the contributions these individuals make to the nation's economy and seeks to provide them with a fair and equitable route towards legal status. The proposed path includes meeting certain requirements, such as background checks, paying taxes, and learning English. This approach aims to address the issue of illegal immigration by providing a viable solution that aligns with American values of inclusivity and fairness.

On the other hand, during his presidency, Donald Trump focused on border security measures as a means to tackle immigration. His administration implemented stricter immigration policies, including the controversial "zero tolerance" policy that led to family separations at the border. Trump's approach aimed to deter illegal immigration by strengthening border enforcement and implementing travel bans. Supporters of this approach argue that it upholds the rule of law and prioritizes national security.

The Biden-Trump showdown on immigration reflects a broader ideological divide within the American electorate. Democrats, viewing immigration as a vital part of the nation's fabric, support Biden's path to citizenship, seeing it as an opportunity to create a more inclusive society that celebrates diversity. Republicans, on the other hand, believe that border security is paramount to protect American jobs and national security.

The immigration issue is not just about policy; it also touches on the American identity and values. The Biden-Trump showdown highlights the contrasting visions for the future of immigration in the United States. As voters, it is essential to consider the impact of these policies on the economy, national security, and social fabric of the country.

Ultimately, the decision on which approach to support rests with the American voters. By examining the accomplishments of Joe Biden and Donald Trump in the realm of immigration, voters can align their choice with their own values and priorities. The outcome of this election will shape the future of immigration policy and determine how the United States engages with the world on this critical issue.

Biden's Immigration Reform Proposal

One of the key issues that has been at the center of the political debate in recent years is immigration. The Biden administration has put forth a comprehensive immigration reform proposal that seeks to address the challenges and complexities of the current system. This proposal has been met with both praise and criticism, depending on one's political beliefs and perspectives.

Biden's immigration reform proposal includes a path to citizenship for the millions of undocumented immigrants living in the United States. This pathway would involve meeting certain requirements, such as background checks, paying taxes, and learning English. The proposal also aims to streamline the legal immigration process, making it more efficient and accessible for those seeking to come to the United States legally.

The proposal also seeks to address the root causes of migration from Central America by investing in the region and providing economic opportunities and support for its people. This approach recognizes that addressing the underlying issues that drive migration is crucial to finding long-term solutions.

Critics of Biden's immigration reform proposal argue that it is too lenient and would encourage illegal immigration. They believe that a strong border security approach, such as the one taken by the Trump administration, is necessary to protect American jobs and national security. They also argue that granting a path to citizenship for undocumented immigrants would be unfair to those who have followed the legal immigration process.

Supporters of the proposal, on the other hand, argue that it is a humane and practical solution to a complex issue. They believe that providing a pathway to citizenship for undocumented immigrants would not only benefit those individuals and their families but also contribute to the economy and strengthen communities. They also argue that addressing the root causes of migration is a more effective approach than simply focusing on border security.

As with many issues, the debate surrounding immigration reform is highly polarized and often driven by political ideology. It is important for American voters to carefully consider the arguments and evidence presented by both sides and make informed decisions based on their own values and priorities.

In the end, the success of Biden's immigration reform proposal will depend on the political will and cooperation of Congress. Only time will tell whether the proposal will become law and whether it will achieve its intended goals of providing a fair and just system for immigrants while protecting the interests of the American people.

Trump's Focus on Border Enforcement

One of the key areas of focus during Donald Trump's presidency was border enforcement. Trump took a tough stance on immigration and implemented several measures aimed at securing the country's borders. This approach was met with mixed reactions, with Republicans praising his efforts to protect national security, while Democrats criticized his policies as harsh and divisive.

Under Trump's administration, border enforcement was a top priority. He promised to build a wall along the U.S.-Mexico border, claiming it would help curb illegal immigration and drug trafficking. Although the construction of the wall faced numerous obstacles and challenges, Trump remained steadfast in his commitment to border security.

In addition to the wall, Trump implemented several other measures to strengthen border enforcement. He increased the number of Border Patrol agents and Immigration and Customs Enforcement (ICE) officers, providing them with additional resources and support. This led to an increase in deportations and removals of undocumented immigrants.

Furthermore, Trump implemented the "Remain in Mexico" policy, which required asylum seekers to wait outside of the United States while their claims were being processed. This policy aimed to discourage illegal entry and reduce the burden on the U.S. immigration system.

Republicans praised Trump's focus on border enforcement, arguing that it was necessary to protect national security and preserve American jobs. They believed that strong border policies would deter illegal immigration and ensure that those entering the country did so legally.

However, Democrats criticized Trump's approach, arguing that it was inhumane and ineffective. They believed that his policies targeted vulnerable populations, such as asylum seekers and undocumented immigrants, and perpetuated a climate of fear and division. Democrats advocated for a more compassionate and comprehensive immigration reform that focused on creating a pathway to citizenship for undocumented immigrants.

As the Biden-Trump showdown unfolds, the issue of border enforcement remains a contentious topic. Joe Biden has promised a more compassionate and inclusive approach to immigration, with a focus on creating a path to citizenship for millions of undocumented immigrants. This stands in stark contrast to Trump's emphasis on border security and enforcement.

The American voters will have to weigh the accomplishments of Trump's focus on border enforcement against Biden's proposed policies. Ultimately, it will be up to the voters to decide which approach aligns with their values and priorities regarding immigration and national security.

Implications for Undocumented Immigrants and National Security

Undocumented immigrants and national security are two intertwined issues that have been at the forefront of political debates for years. The

Biden-Trump showdown presents contrasting perspectives on how to address these complex challenges, with Democrats and Republicans offering divergent approaches and policies.

For Democrats, under President Joe Biden's leadership, there is a clear commitment to finding a path to citizenship for undocumented immigrants. Biden's comprehensive immigration reform proposal aims to provide a pathway to citizenship for the estimated 11 million undocumented immigrants living in the United States. This approach recognizes the contributions and potential of these individuals, seeking to integrate them into society and provide them with the rights and protections they deserve.

From a Republican perspective, former President Donald Trump took a different approach, focusing on border security measures as a means to address national security concerns. Trump's administration implemented strict immigration policies, including the controversial family separation policy, to deter unauthorized border crossings. The emphasis was on fortifying the borders and enforcing existing immigration laws.

The implications of these divergent approaches for undocumented immigrants are significant. Under Biden's plan, millions of undocumented immigrants would have the opportunity to come out of the shadows, pursue legal status, and eventually become citizens. This would not only provide them with a pathway to a better life but also enable them to fully contribute to the American economy and society.

However, Republicans argue that a more lenient approach to immigration could have potential national security implications. They believe that stricter border security measures are necessary to prevent potential threats from entering the country. From their perspective, undocumented immigrants may pose risks to national security, and therefore, a more cautious and restrictive approach is required.

Ultimately, the implications for undocumented immigrants and national security depend on which approach is prioritized. Democrats emphasize the need for comprehensive immigration reform, focusing on integrating undocumented immigrants into society, while Republicans prioritize border security measures as a means to protect national security.

As American voters, it is crucial to consider the implications of these contrasting perspectives. The Biden-Trump showdown offers us a platform to assess the potential impact of different policies on both undocumented immigrants and national security. By understanding the implications of these approaches, we can make informed decisions that align with our values and priorities as citizens of the United States.

COVID-19 Response: Biden's Vaccination Plan vs. Trump's Operation Warp Speed

In the wake of the global COVID-19 pandemic, the United States faced an unprecedented crisis that demanded swift and effective action. The American voters witnessed two distinct approaches to tackling the virus – Joe Biden's Vaccination Plan and Donald Trump's Operation Warp Speed.

Joe Biden, the 46th President of the United States, entered office with a clear vision to combat the virus. Biden's Vaccination Plan aimed to expedite the distribution of vaccines and ensure equitable access for all Americans. Recognizing the importance of a coordinated response, Biden pledged to work closely with state and local governments, as well as public health experts, to streamline the vaccination process. His plan prioritized the most vulnerable populations, such as healthcare workers, the elderly, and those with underlying health conditions. By establishing vaccination sites across the country and mobilizing the Federal Emergency Management Agency (FEMA) and the National Guard, Biden aimed to administer 100 million vaccine doses within his first 100 days in office.

On the other hand, Donald Trump's Operation Warp Speed, initiated during his tenure as president, focused on the rapid development and production of vaccines. Trump's administration collaborated with pharmaceutical companies, providing funding and regulatory support to expedite the vaccine development process. Operation Warp Speed successfully delivered vaccines within record time, enabling millions of Americans to receive protection against the virus. However, critics argued that the distribution efforts fell short, with some states experiencing shortages and logistical challenges.

While both approaches shared the common goal of vaccinating the American population, Biden's plan emphasized a more comprehensive and inclusive strategy. He recognized the importance of addressing the underlying disparities that the pandemic had exposed, particularly in communities of color. By prioritizing equity and accessibility, Biden's plan aimed to bridge these gaps and ensure that no American was left behind.

The American voters must evaluate these two approaches based on their effectiveness, efficiency, and impact. Biden's Vaccination Plan provides a roadmap for a more inclusive and coordinated response, addressing the concerns of the most vulnerable populations. Trump's Operation Warp Speed, on the other hand, demonstrated the ability to develop vaccines at an unprecedented pace but faced criticism for the challenges in distribution.

As the nation continues its battle against the virus, it is crucial for the American voters to critically analyze and assess the COVID-19 response strategies employed by both administrations. Understanding the strengths and weaknesses of each approach will contribute to informed decision-making and pave the way for more effective crisis management in the future.

Biden's Efforts to Accelerate Vaccine Distribution

In the face of one of the greatest public health crises in recent history, President Joe Biden has made it his top priority to accelerate the distribution of COVID-19 vaccines across the nation. Recognizing the urgent need to get vaccines into the arms of Americans, Biden has implemented a comprehensive strategy that aims to bring an end to the pandemic and restore normalcy to our lives.

One of the key pillars of Biden's vaccination plan is to increase the production, supply, and distribution of vaccines. The President has worked tirelessly to secure enough doses to vaccinate every American, negotiating contracts with vaccine manufacturers to ramp up production. Through his efforts, the United States has secured millions of doses, ensuring that there is a sufficient supply to meet the demand.

To ensure an efficient and equitable distribution process, Biden has established community vaccination centers across the country. These centers, strategically located in underserved communities, aim to reach those who have been disproportionately affected by the virus. By prioritizing vulnerable populations, including the elderly and essential workers, Biden's plan seeks to address the systemic inequities that have exacerbated the impact of the pandemic on marginalized communities.

Additionally, Biden has implemented a robust public education campaign to combat vaccine hesitancy. Recognizing that widespread vaccination is crucial to achieving herd immunity, the President has enlisted the help of trusted voices, including healthcare professionals and community leaders, to encourage Americans to get vaccinated. By addressing misinformation and promoting the safety and efficacy of the vaccines, Biden aims to build public confidence in the vaccination process.

Furthermore, Biden has prioritized the global fight against COVID-19 by rejoining the World Health Organization and pledging support to international vaccine distribution efforts. Recognizing that the virus knows no borders, Biden understands the importance of working together with other nations to combat the pandemic on a global scale.

Through his unwavering commitment to accelerating vaccine distribution, President Joe Biden has demonstrated strong leadership and a clear vision for ending the COVID-19 pandemic. His comprehensive strategy, which includes increasing production and supply, establishing community vaccination centers, addressing vaccine hesitancy, and prioritizing global cooperation, aims to bring relief to the American people and restore stability to our nation. With Biden at the helm, there is hope that we can overcome this crisis and emerge stronger than ever before.

Trump's Approach to Vaccine Development

One of the most critical issues facing the American people is the development and distribution of a COVID-19 vaccine. In this section, we will explore Donald Trump's approach to vaccine development and how it differs from Joe Biden's perspective.

Donald Trump's administration launched Operation Warp Speed, a program aimed at accelerating the development, production, and distribution of a safe and effective vaccine. With a goal of delivering 300 million doses of a vaccine by January 2021, the Trump administration mobilized resources and partnered with pharmaceutical companies to expedite the process. This approach focused on fast-tracking the regulatory process and removing bureaucratic hurdles to ensure a timely response to the pandemic.

Critics argue that Trump's approach to vaccine development was driven by political motivations rather than sound scientific judgment. They claim that the administration prioritized speed over safety, raising concerns about the potential for compromised efficacy. However, supporters argue that Operation Warp Speed successfully brought multiple vaccines to the final stages of development in record time, demonstrating the efficacy of Trump's approach.

Furthermore, Trump's administration negotiated agreements with pharmaceutical companies to secure millions of vaccine doses in advance, ensuring that the American people would have access to a vaccine as soon as it became available. This proactive approach aimed to prevent a shortage and prioritize the health and safety of American citizens.

However, it is important to note that Trump's approach to vaccine development was not without challenges. There were concerns about the politicization of the vaccine approval process, as the administration faced accusations of pressuring the FDA and CDC to expedite the approval and distribution of a vaccine before the 2020 presidential election. These allegations raised doubts about the transparency and integrity of the vaccine development process.

In contrast to Trump's approach, Joe Biden has emphasized the importance of scientific integrity and transparency in vaccine development. Biden's plan focuses on ensuring that any vaccine approved for distribution undergoes rigorous testing and meets the highest safety standards. He has pledged to rely on the guidance of public health experts and restore trust in the vaccine development process.

As American voters, it is crucial to consider the approaches of both candidates when evaluating their ability to navigate the challenges posed by the COVID-19 pandemic. The development and distribution of a vaccine will play a vital role in controlling the spread of the virus and restoring normalcy in our lives.

Effects on Public Health and Pandemic Management

The COVID-19 pandemic has had a profound impact on public health and the way it is managed. In this section, we will examine the approaches taken by President Joe Biden and former President Donald Trump in addressing this unprecedented crisis.

Under President Biden's leadership, there has been a significant shift in the federal government's response to the pandemic. One of the key aspects of Biden's approach is his commitment to science and evidence-based decision making. He has established a COVID-19 task force composed of leading experts and has consistently relied on their guidance to shape his policies. This has resulted in a more coordinated and effective response to the pandemic, with a focus on testing, contact tracing, and vaccination efforts.

Biden's vaccination plan has been particularly noteworthy. He set an ambitious goal of administering 100 million doses within his first 100 days in office, and not only did he achieve that goal, but he also surpassed it. His administration has worked tirelessly to ramp up vaccine production and distribution, partnering with private sector companies to establish vaccination sites across the country. This has played a crucial role in accelerating the pace of vaccinations and bringing us closer to achieving herd immunity.

In contrast, former President Trump's approach to the pandemic was marked by a lack of coordination and a disregard for scientific advice. His administration downplayed the severity of the virus in its early stages and did not implement a cohesive national strategy. While the development of vaccines under Operation Warp Speed was commendable, the distribution and administration of vaccines were not effectively managed, leading to delays and confusion.

The effects of these differing approaches on public health have been significant. Under Biden's leadership, there has been a decline in new COVID-19 cases, hospitalizations, and deaths. Vaccination rates have steadily increased, and there is a sense of hope and optimism as we move closer to ending the pandemic.

On the other hand, Trump's handling of the pandemic has been criticized for contributing to the severity of the crisis. The lack of a unified approach and inconsistent messaging resulted in confusion and mistrust among the American public. This, in turn, led to higher infection rates and a greater strain on the healthcare system.

In conclusion, the effects of public health and pandemic management under Biden and Trump have been starkly different. Biden's emphasis on science, coordination, and vaccination efforts has led to a more effective response to the pandemic and a path towards recovery. Trump's approach, characterized by a lack of coordination and a disregard for scientific advice, contributed to the severity of the crisis. As American voters, it is crucial to consider these contrasting approaches and their impact on public health when evaluating the accomplishments of Biden and Trump.

Education: Biden's Push for Free Community College vs. Trump's Focus on School Choice

In the ongoing battle for the future of American education, Joe Biden and Donald Trump have presented contrasting visions. Biden's proposal for free community college aims to expand access to higher education and provide opportunities for all Americans to gain the skills they need to succeed in the modern workforce. On the other hand, Trump's focus on school choice emphasizes the importance of empowering parents to make decisions about their children's education, including the option to attend charter schools or use vouchers for private schools.

For Democrats, Biden's push for free community college is seen as a progressive step towards creating a more equitable society. They argue that education is a fundamental right and that everyone should have the opportunity to pursue higher education without the burden of crippling student loan debt. By investing in community colleges, Biden aims to provide affordable education and job training programs that can lead to well-paying jobs and economic mobility.

Republicans, on the other hand, support Trump's focus on school choice as a means to increase competition and improve the quality of education. They argue that parents should have the freedom to choose the best educational environment for their children, whether it be a traditional public school, charter school, or private school. Trump's administration advocated for expanding charter schools and implementing voucher programs, which they believe will drive innovation and accountability in the education system.

Both approaches have their merits and drawbacks. Biden's proposal for free community college has the potential to level the playing field and address socio-economic disparities in access to higher education. However, critics argue that it may not be financially sustainable and could lead to increased taxes or government spending. On the other hand, Trump's focus on school choice may provide more options for parents and students, but there are concerns about the quality and accountability of charter schools and the potential for further segregating the education system.

As American voters, it is crucial to carefully consider the impact of these education policies on our society and the future of our children. Education is the key to unlocking opportunities and building a strong economy. Whether we support Biden's push for free community college or Trump's focus on school choice, it is essential to prioritize investment in education and ensure that all Americans have access to quality educational opportunities that prepare them for success in the 21st century.

Biden's Proposal for Expanding Access to Higher Education

In his bid for the presidency, Joe Biden has put forth a comprehensive plan to expand access to higher education for all Americans. Recognizing the importance of a college degree in today's competitive job market, Biden's proposal seeks to address the rising costs of tuition and the burden of student loan debt that many Americans face.

One key aspect of Biden's plan is his commitment to making community college tuition-free for all students. This initiative aims to provide affordable education and training to individuals seeking to acquire the skills necessary for well-paying jobs. By removing the financial barrier that often prevents students from pursuing higher education, Biden hopes to level the playing field and ensure that all Americans have the opportunity to succeed.

Furthermore, Biden's proposal includes plans to double the maximum Pell Grant award, which would provide low-income students with additional financial support to cover the cost of tuition, books, and living expenses. This increase in funding would enable more students to attend college without the burden of overwhelming debt.

In addition to making college more affordable, Biden plans to invest in historically Black colleges and universities (HBCUs) and minority-serving institutions (MSIs). These institutions play a crucial role in providing quality education to underrepresented communities, and Biden's proposal recognizes the need for increased funding and support to ensure their continued success.

To address the issue of student loan debt, Biden plans to implement income-driven repayment plans and streamline the Public Service Loan Forgiveness program. These measures would help alleviate the financial strain faced by graduates and encourage individuals to pursue careers in public service, education, and other fields that benefit society as a whole.

Biden's proposal for expanding access to higher education is a testament to his commitment to creating opportunities for all Americans. By making college more affordable and reducing the burden of student loan debt, Biden aims to empower individuals to pursue their dreams and contribute to the economic growth and prosperity of our nation.

As American voters, it is important to consider Biden's plan for expanding access to higher education in relation to his other policy proposals. By examining his stance on economic policies, foreign relations, climate change, racial equality, healthcare, immigration, COVID-19 response, criminal justice reform, and the Supreme Court, we can gain a comprehensive understanding of Biden's vision for our country and make an informed decision in the upcoming election.

Trump's Emphasis on Education Vouchers

Education has always been a crucial topic in American politics, and it is no different when it comes to the perspectives of Democrats and Republicans. In this section, we will explore Donald Trump's emphasis on education vouchers, a policy that differed greatly from Joe Biden's approach.

Donald Trump believed in empowering parents and students to choose the best education options for themselves. One of the ways he sought to achieve this was through education vouchers. These vouchers would provide families with public funds to be used towards private or charter schools of their choice, allowing them to opt out of underperforming public schools. Trump argued that this would increase competition and drive improvements in public schools, as they would have to compete for students.

Trump's emphasis on education vouchers was seen as a way to promote school choice and give parents more control over their children's education. Advocates of this policy argue that it can help address educational inequalities and provide opportunities for students in disadvantaged areas. By introducing competition into the education system, Trump believed that schools would be incentivized to improve their quality, leading to better outcomes for all students.

However, critics of education vouchers expressed concerns about the potential negative impacts on public schools. They argued that diverting public funds to private schools could undermine the already limited resources available to public education. Additionally, opponents raised concerns about accountability and the potential for discrimination in private schools that could receive public funding.

From a Republican perspective, Trump's emphasis on education vouchers aligned with their belief in limited government intervention and individual choice. They saw it as a way to empower parents and students, giving them the freedom to choose the best educational path for themselves.

On the other hand, Democrats, including Joe Biden, have traditionally been more supportive of public education and increasing funding for public schools. Biden's approach to education focused on expanding access to free community college and investing in public schools to ensure equal opportunities for all students.

In conclusion, Trump's emphasis on education vouchers represented a departure from the traditional Democratic approach to education. While it aimed to promote school choice and empower parents, it also raised concerns about the potential consequences for public schools. Understanding the different perspectives on this issue is crucial for American voters as they consider the accomplishments and policies of both Donald Trump and Joe Biden in the realm of education.

Impact on Educational Equity and Funding

One of the crucial areas where the policies and approaches of Joe Biden and Donald Trump diverge significantly is in the realm of education. Both candidates have distinct perspectives on how to address educational equity and funding, which has a direct impact on the future of American students.

Under Joe Biden's leadership, there is a strong emphasis on expanding educational opportunities and ensuring equity in access to quality education. Biden has proposed a bold plan to make two years of community college free for all Americans, including those from low-income backgrounds. This initiative aims to remove financial barriers that often hinder students from pursuing higher education and acquiring the skills needed for well-paying jobs. By providing free community college, Biden's plan would not only empower individuals but also boost the overall competitiveness and productivity of the American workforce.

In contrast, Donald Trump's approach to education focuses more on school choice and competition. Trump supports the expansion of charter schools and voucher programs, which allow parents to choose the school their child attends, including private schools. Proponents argue that this approach promotes healthy competition and forces schools to improve, thereby benefiting students. However, critics argue that such policies can exacerbate educational inequities, as they may result in the diversion of resources and funding away from public schools that serve a majority of disadvantaged students.

Furthermore, Biden's commitment to educational equity extends beyond college affordability. He aims to increase funding for public schools, particularly those in low-income areas, to ensure that every child receives a quality education regardless of their zip code. Biden also seeks to invest in early childhood education, recognizing the critical role it plays in setting a strong foundation for children's future success.

On the other hand, Trump's policies have focused more on reducing the federal government's role in education and empowering states and local communities to make decisions. While this approach may promote flexibility and local control, it raises concerns about potential disparities in educational resources and opportunities, particularly for marginalized communities.

In conclusion, the impact of the Biden-Trump showdown on educational equity and funding is significant. Biden's focus on expanding access to higher education, increasing funding for public schools, and investing in early childhood education aligns with a vision of creating a more equitable and prosperous future. Conversely, Trump's emphasis on school choice and reducing federal intervention in education reflects a different approach that prioritizes competition and local decision-making. The choice between these two perspectives will have far-reaching consequences for the educational opportunities and outcomes of American students. As American voters, it is crucial to carefully consider these divergent approaches and the potential impact they will have on the future of education in our country.

Criminal Justice Reform: Biden's Efforts for Police Accountability vs. Trump's Tough-on-Crime Approach

In the ongoing battle between Joe Biden and Donald Trump, one of the most important issues at stake is criminal justice reform. The approaches taken by these two candidates couldn't be more different. Biden's efforts for police accountability stand in stark contrast to Trump's tough-on-crime approach.

Joe Biden, a Democrat, has long been an advocate for criminal justice reform. He believes in addressing the systemic issues within law enforcement that have led to the mistreatment and abuse of marginalized communities. Biden's plan includes implementing policies that promote police accountability, such as requiring body cameras, banning chokeholds, and establishing a national database to track police misconduct. He also supports the demilitarization of police departments and the redirection of funds towards community-based programs that address the root causes of crime.

On the other hand, Donald Trump, a Republican, has often taken a tough-on-crime stance. He has advocated for increased police presence and harsher sentencing for offenders. Trump's approach prioritizes law and order, often at the expense of addressing the underlying issues that contribute to crime. While he has made efforts to support law enforcement, critics argue that his approach fails to address the systemic problems within the criminal justice system and perpetuates the cycle of mass incarceration.

The American voters must carefully consider the implications of these approaches. Biden's efforts for police accountability have the potential to rebuild trust between communities and law enforcement, ensuring that all citizens are treated with fairness and respect. By redirecting resources towards community-based initiatives, Biden's plan aims to address the root causes of crime and help individuals reintegrate into society.

On the other hand, Trump's tough-on-crime approach may provide a sense of security, but it risks perpetuating a broken system that disproportionately affects marginalized communities. Critics argue that this approach fails to address the underlying issues that contribute to crime and does little to promote long-term solutions.

Ultimately, the choice between Biden's efforts for police accountability and Trump's tough-on-crime approach comes down to the fundamental values of fairness, justice, and equality. The American voters must carefully consider which approach aligns with their vision for a more just and equitable society.

Biden's Initiatives for Police Reform and Accountability

In recent years, issues of police misconduct, racial profiling, and excessive use of force have sparked nationwide protests and calls for reform. President Joe Biden has made it a priority to address these concerns and restore trust between law enforcement and the communities they serve. Through a series of initiatives, Biden aims to bring about meaningful police reform and ensure accountability within the criminal justice system.

One of the key pillars of Biden's approach to police reform is the implementation of comprehensive training programs. The president recognizes the importance of equipping law enforcement officers with the necessary tools and tactics to de-escalate situations and avoid the use of excessive force. By investing in training that emphasizes community policing and nonviolent conflict resolution, Biden aims to foster positive relationships between police officers and the communities they protect.

Another crucial aspect of Biden's initiatives is the promotion of transparency and accountability. The president supports the establishment of national standards for the use of force, as well as the mandatory use of body cameras by all law enforcement officers. These measures serve to ensure that incidents of misconduct are properly documented and can be thoroughly investigated. Moreover, Biden has expressed his commitment to holding officers accountable for their actions by supporting the prosecution of those who violate the law.

In addition to these measures, Biden acknowledges the need for systemic changes within the criminal justice system. He supports the end of mandatory minimum sentences for nonviolent offenses, as well as the elimination of racial disparities in sentencing. By addressing these issues, Biden aims to create a fair and just system that treats all individuals equally, regardless of their race or socioeconomic background.

Furthermore, Biden recognizes the importance of addressing the root causes of crime and investing in community resources. He advocates for increased funding for social programs, education, and mental health services. By providing individuals with the support they need, Biden aims to reduce crime rates and create safer communities.

Overall, Biden's initiatives for police reform and accountability represent a comprehensive and thoughtful approach to addressing the concerns of the American people. By prioritizing training, transparency, and accountability, he aims to restore trust and ensure that law enforcement serves and protects all communities. Through these efforts, Biden seeks to create a criminal justice system that is fair, just, and equitable for all.

Trump's Focus on Law and Order

Section: Trump's Focus on Law and Order

Introduction:

In the ongoing battle for the presidency, one of the key aspects that separates Joe Biden and Donald Trump is their approach to law and order. While Biden emphasizes the need for police accountability and social justice, Trump takes a tough-on-crime stance. This section delves into Trump's focus on law and order, highlighting his policies and actions that aimed to maintain public safety and protect American communities.

Law and Order Policies:

Donald Trump, during his tenure as president, made law and order a cornerstone of his administration. Recognizing the importance of safeguarding American citizens, Trump implemented several policies to combat crime and uphold the rule of law. He prioritized the safety and security of communities by advocating for stricter immigration policies, enhancing border security measures, and pursuing tough penalties for drug traffickers and violent offenders.

Border Security:

Under Trump's leadership, significant efforts were made to secure the country's borders. He prioritized building a wall along the southern border, aiming to curb illegal immigration and drug trafficking. Trump's border security initiatives were intended to protect American jobs and prevent potential threats from entering the country. His supporters argue that these measures were crucial to maintaining law and order.

Tough-on-Crime Approach:

Trump's tough-on-crime stance resonated with many Americans who believed in a robust criminal justice system. He advocated for harsh penalties for drug offenses, targeting drug cartels and combating the opioid crisis. Trump's emphasis on law and order included supporting law enforcement agencies and providing them with the necessary resources to combat crime effectively.

Support for Police:

Throughout his presidency, Trump consistently expressed his support for law enforcement officers and their dedication to protecting communities. He condemned violence against police officers and advocated for increased funding to support their efforts. Trump's focus on law and order included initiatives to improve police training and equipment, ensuring that they have the necessary resources to perform their duties efficiently.

Conclusion:

Donald Trump's focus on law and order was a central aspect of his presidency. His policies and actions aimed to protect American communities, strengthen border security, and support law enforcement agencies. While his tough-on-crime approach garnered support from his Republican base, it also sparked criticism from those who believed in the need for police accountability and criminal justice reform. As American voters weigh their options, Trump's law and order stance remains a defining characteristic of his presidency.

Consequences for Criminal Justice System and Communities

The criminal justice system and the communities it serves are of crucial importance in any society. The decisions made by political leaders can have a profound impact on the effectiveness and fairness of this system, as well as on the safety and well-being of communities. In this section, we will explore the consequences of the Biden-Trump showdown on the criminal justice system and communities, examining the different approaches taken by Joe Biden and Donald Trump.

Biden's Efforts for Police Accountability

Joe Biden has long been an advocate for police reform and accountability. He understands the need to address systemic issues within law enforcement and to rebuild trust between police officers and the communities they serve. As president, Biden has committed to implementing much-needed reforms, such as banning chokeholds, establishing a national use of force standard, and providing funding for police training on de-escalation techniques and implicit bias. These efforts are aimed at promoting transparency, accountability, and community-oriented policing.

Trump's Tough-on-Crime Approach

Donald Trump, on the other hand, has taken a tough-on-crime approach during his presidency. He has emphasized the need for law and order, advocating for stricter sentencing and increased police presence in communities. While this approach may aim to deter crime, it has also raised concerns about over-policing and disproportionately affecting marginalized communities. Trump's administration has been criticized for its lack of focus on police reform and addressing systemic issues within the criminal justice system.

Impacts on Communities

The consequences of these differing approaches are felt directly by the communities affected by the criminal justice system. Biden's efforts for police accountability and reform are seen by many as a step towards addressing longstanding issues of racial bias and excessive use of force. By promoting transparency and community engagement, Biden's approach seeks to rebuild trust between law enforcement and communities, fostering safer and more inclusive neighborhoods.

Trump's tough-on-crime approach, while aiming to prioritize public safety, has raised concerns about the potential for increased racial profiling and the perpetuation of systemic injustices. Critics argue that this approach fails to address the underlying causes of crime and may further alienate marginalized communities.

Conclusion

The consequences of the Biden-Trump showdown on the criminal justice system and communities are significant. Biden's commitment to police accountability and reform offers the potential for a more equitable and effective justice system, one that prioritizes community engagement and safety. Trump's tough-on-crime approach, however, raises concerns about the potential for increased racial bias and systemic injustices. As American voters, it is important to consider these consequences when evaluating the accomplishments and approaches of Joe Biden and Donald Trump in relation to criminal justice reform and community well-being.

Supreme Court: Biden's Potential Expansion vs. Trump's Conservative Appointments

The Supreme Court holds immense power in shaping the direction of our country, making the appointment of justices a crucial decision for any president. In the ongoing battle between Joe Biden and Donald Trump, their choices for the Supreme Court reflect their respective ideologies and priorities.

Joe Biden has expressed his intention to potentially expand the Supreme Court if elected, a move that has divided opinions among the American voters. Biden believes that expanding the court could help balance the conservative majority that currently exists. Democrats argue that this expansion is necessary to ensure a more diverse and representative judiciary that reflects the values and concerns of the American people. They point to issues such as reproductive rights, LGBTQ+ rights, and voting rights, where they believe a conservative-leaning court could hinder progress.

On the other hand, Donald Trump's appointments of conservative justices, such as Brett Kavanaugh and Amy Coney Barrett, have been celebrated by Republicans. Trump's strategy was to solidify a conservative majority in the court, hoping to influence decisions on issues like abortion, gun rights, and religious freedom. Republicans believe that a conservative-leaning court is essential to protecting traditional values and upholding the Constitution.

The battle over Supreme Court appointments has become increasingly partisan, with both sides recognizing the long-lasting impact these appointments can have on the nation's laws and policies. The stakes are high, and the American voters must consider the potential consequences of these appointments on the issues they care about most.

Ultimately, the Supreme Court will play a critical role in shaping the future of our country, regardless of who wins the presidency. The decisions made by the justices will impact issues such as healthcare, immigration, criminal justice reform, and much more. It is essential for the American voters to educate themselves on the judicial philosophies of the candidates and understand the potential implications of their appointments.

In the end, the battle between Biden's potential expansion of the Supreme Court and Trump's conservative appointments reflects the larger ideological divide in our nation. The American voters must carefully consider which approach aligns with their values and priorities as they make their decision in this critical election. The future of the Supreme Court and the direction of our country hang in the balance.

Biden's Consideration of Court Expansion

The discussion surrounding the potential expansion of the Supreme Court has become a significant point of interest in the Biden administration. This section will delve into the implications of this consideration and how it differs from Trump's approach to appointing conservative justices.

Joe Biden, as seen by Democrats, has long been an advocate for progressive policies and social justice. One area where he has faced criticism from his own party is his stance on the Supreme Court. Many Democrats argue that the court has become heavily conservative, tipping the scales in favor of conservative ideologies for years to come. In response to this, Biden has expressed openness to exploring the idea of court expansion.

The concept of expanding the Supreme Court involves increasing the number of justices beyond the current nine. Proponents of this idea argue that it would help restore balance to the court, ensuring a more diverse range of perspectives and preventing any one ideology from dominating.

On the other hand, Trump's approach to the Supreme Court was focused on appointing conservative justices who aligned with his own beliefs.

Throughout his presidency, he successfully appointed three conservative justices, shifting the balance of the court toward a more conservative majority.

The consideration of court expansion by Biden presents a stark contrast to Trump's conservative appointments. While Trump sought to solidify conservative control over the court, Biden is contemplating measures to address the perceived imbalance and allow for a more equitable representation of ideas.

However, it is important to note that court expansion is a contentious and complex issue. Critics argue that it would undermine the independence and integrity of the judiciary, suggesting that it could be seen as a partisan move. They argue that expanding the court solely for ideological reasons could set a dangerous precedent, leading to a cycle of court packing every time the balance of power shifts.

As American voters, it is crucial to understand and evaluate the potential consequences of court expansion. This section aims to provide an overview of the debate surrounding this topic, allowing readers to form their own opinions on whether Biden's consideration of court expansion is a necessary step toward a more balanced judiciary or a politically motivated maneuver.

Trump's Nominations of Conservative Justices

Section: Trump's Nominations of Conservative Justices

In the realm of Supreme Court nominations, few issues carry as much weight as the appointment of justices who will shape the direction of the nation's highest court for decades to come. Throughout his presidency, Donald Trump seized the opportunity to reshape the Supreme Court by nominating conservative justices, a move that garnered both praise and criticism.

Trump's commitment to nominating conservative justices aligned with the values and priorities of his Republican base. For conservatives, these nominations represented a chance to solidify a conservative majority on the Court and potentially influence landmark decisions on key issues such as abortion, gun rights, and religious liberties.

With the appointments of Justices Neil Gorsuch, Brett Kavanaugh, and Amy Coney Barrett, Trump successfully fulfilled his promise of nominating conservative justices. These nominations were celebrated by Republicans who believed that a conservative Court would preserve and uphold their core values and principles.

For Republicans, these justices were seen as a bulwark against what they perceived as a liberal overreach in the courts. They believed that these nominees would interpret the Constitution as it was originally intended, adhering to a strict constructionist approach.

However, Democrats expressed concerns about the impact of these conservative appointments on issues such as reproductive rights, LGBTQ+ rights, voting rights, and healthcare. They feared that these justices would vote to overturn or chip away at landmark decisions such as Roe v. Wade, Obergefell v. Hodges, and the Affordable Care Act.

The nominations of conservative justices by Trump further deepened the ideological divide within the Supreme Court. With these appointments, the Court shifted to the right, and many anticipated that this shift would have significant implications for future decisions.

The impact of these conservative appointments will likely be felt for years, if not decades, to come. As the Court takes up cases that have far-reaching consequences on issues central to the American public, the conservative majority is poised to shape the legal landscape in a manner consistent with their judicial philosophies.

The nominations of conservative justices by Trump underscore the importance of the Supreme Court in shaping the direction of the nation. As voters, it is crucial to consider the potential impact of these nominations on the issues that matter most to us, whether it be reproductive rights, LGBTQ+ rights, or the interpretation of the Constitution.

In the Biden-Trump showdown, the nominations of conservative justices by Trump represent a stark contrast to Biden's potential approach to the Supreme Court. As voters, we must critically evaluate the implications of these appointments and decide which vision of the Court aligns best with our values and priorities.

Implications for Judicial Balance and Policy Direction

The Biden-Trump Showdown: A Democratic and Republican Perspective on Accomplishments

Addressed to: THE AMERICAN VOTERS

Niche: ACCOMPLISHMENTS OF JOE BIDEN AS SEEN BY DEMOCRATS AND OF DONALD TRUMP BY REPUBLICANS

In this section, we will explore the implications for judicial balance and policy direction under the leadership of Joe Biden and Donald Trump. Both presidents had different approaches and visions when it came to shaping the judiciary and setting the policy direction of the country.

One of the key areas where Biden and Trump diverged was in their Supreme Court appointments. Biden's potential expansion of the Supreme Court represents a shift towards a more liberal and progressive judiciary. This expansion, if implemented, could have far-reaching implications for the balance of power within the court and the interpretation of the Constitution.

On the other hand, Trump's conservative appointments to the Supreme Court aimed to solidify a conservative majority and a more strict interpretation of the law. This approach aligns with his overall policy direction and desire to roll back certain progressive policies implemented during the Obama era.

The implications of these differing approaches are significant. Biden's potential expansion could lead to a more liberal court that is more likely to uphold policies that promote social justice, civil rights, and environmental protection. On the contrary, Trump's conservative appointments may result in a court that is more inclined to support policies that prioritize individual liberties, limited government intervention, and conservative values.

Furthermore, the judicial balance and policy direction extend beyond the Supreme Court. Biden's commitment to social justice and police accountability may shape lower court appointments, leading to a judiciary that is more receptive to civil rights and criminal justice reform. Conversely, Trump's tough-on-crime approach and emphasis on law and order may have influenced his lower court appointments to prioritize a more conservative and punitive approach to criminal justice.

The implications for judicial balance and policy direction go beyond the courtroom. The decisions made by these courts will shape the future of our nation, from healthcare and immigration to climate change and racial equality. As American voters, it is essential to consider how each candidate's judicial appointments and policy direction align with our values and the direction we want our country to take.

In conclusion, the implications for judicial balance and policy direction under Biden and Trump are vast. The potential expansion of the Supreme Court under Biden could lead to a more progressive judiciary, while Trump's conservative appointments aimed to solidify a strict interpretation of the law. These decisions have far-reaching consequences for the future of our nation, and it is vital for American voters to evaluate the impact of these choices on the issues that matter most to them.

Conclusion: Evaluating the Biden-Trump Showdown from the American Voters' Perspective

Throughout the Biden-Trump showdown, the American voters have witnessed a fierce battle between two political giants, each representing a distinct set of values and priorities. From the accomplishments of Joe Biden as seen by Democrats to the accomplishments of Donald Trump as seen by Republicans, this section aimed to evaluate the key policy areas that shaped their presidencies.

One of the most significant differences between the two administrations was their approach to economic policies. Biden focused on job creation strategies, aiming to stimulate the economy and uplift the American workforce. On the other hand, Trump's tax cuts aimed to boost businesses and promote economic growth. American voters were divided on which approach was more effective in fostering sustainable economic development.

Foreign relations also played a crucial role in the Biden-Trump showdown. Biden's diplomatic approach emphasized multilateralism and collaboration with international allies, in contrast to Trump's "America First" doctrine. While Biden's approach aimed to rebuild international relationships and restore America's standing in the world, Trump's policies prioritized national interests and protectionism.

Another key area of contention was climate change. Biden's clean energy agenda sought to address the pressing issue of global warming and recommit the United States to the Paris Agreement. On the other hand, Trump's decision to withdraw from the agreement reflected his administration's skepticism towards international climate efforts.

American voters had to decide which approach aligned better with their environmental concerns and long-term sustainability goals.

Racial equality emerged as a critical issue during the Biden-Trump showdown. Biden's commitment to social justice and police accountability stood in contrast to Trump's "law and order" stance. American voters had to weigh the importance of addressing systemic racism and promoting racial equality against concerns of public safety and law enforcement.

Healthcare was another polarizing issue between the two administrations. Biden aimed to expand the Affordable Care Act, ensuring greater access to affordable healthcare. In contrast, Trump sought to repeal and replace the ACA, advocating for a more market-driven approach. The American voters had to consider the impact of these opposing healthcare strategies on their own wellbeing and that of their fellow citizens.

The immigration debate also took center stage during the showdown. Biden's path to citizenship offered a more inclusive and humanitarian approach, while Trump's border security measures prioritized national security. Voters had to decide whether they valued compassion and inclusivity or strict border control.

The COVID-19 response also significantly influenced the voters' perspective. Biden's vaccination plan aimed to accelerate the distribution of vaccines and curb the pandemic's impact. In contrast, Trump's Operation Warp Speed focused on fast-tracking vaccine development. American voters assessed which approach they believed would effectively combat the virus and protect public health.

Education and criminal justice reform were additional areas of contention. Biden advocated for free community college and prioritized education as a means of economic empowerment. Trump, on the other hand, focused on school choice, emphasizing the importance of individual liberty and parental rights. When it came to criminal justice reform, Biden's efforts for police accountability were contrasted with Trump's tough-on-crime approach. Voters had to determine which policies aligned better with their values of equality, justice, and personal freedom.

Lastly, the Supreme Court became a significant battleground during the Biden-Trump showdown. Biden's potential expansion of the court aimed to rebalance its ideological composition, while Trump's conservative appointments aimed to solidify a conservative majority. The American voters had to consider the long-term implications of these appointments on issues such as reproductive rights, LGBTQ+ rights, and gun control.

In conclusion, the Biden-Trump showdown brought to the forefront a multitude of policy differences that shaped their presidencies. American voters had to critically evaluate where their priorities lay within the realms of economic policies, foreign relations, climate change, racial equality, healthcare, immigration, COVID-19 response, education, criminal justice reform, and the Supreme Court. Ultimately, the voters' perspective on these accomplishments would determine the direction of the nation for years to come.